NEW WAY

A cat called Tim

by
Anne Oates

Illustrated by
Barry Wilkinson

Macmillan Education

Editorial Consultant: Donna Bailey

First published 1987
Reprinted 1988, 1991

Published by
MACMILLAN EDUCATION LTD
Houndmills, Basingstoke, Hampshire RG21 2XS
and London
Companies and representatives
throughout the world

Cover design by The Design Works, Reading

Printed in Hong Kong

British Library Cataloguing in Publication Data
Oates, Ann
A cat called Tim.—(New Way)
I. Title II. Dowland, David III. Smith,
Joyce IV. Series
428.6   PE1119
ISBN 0–333–41896–4

Chapter 1: The twins want a pet

"I'm not going to school any more," said Andrew when he got off the bus.

"Nor am I," said Carol.

"I'm not going to school at all," said David in his push-chair.

"Oh dear," said Mum. "Not again! Now what is the matter? Something bad must have happened. Let's go home and you can tell me all about it."

As soon as they got home, Mum made a pot of tea. Andrew got the biscuit tin, Carol put some cushions on the floor, and David banged his drum.

"Now," said Mum when they were all settled. "Drink your tea and tell me all about it."

Andrew and Carol looked at each other and said both together, "Today we had to write about a pet. How can we write about a pet when you won't let us have one?"

"So we can't go to school ever again," they said.

"That is difficult," said Mum. "But it is sometimes difficult when you have a pet. I don't know what we can do about it. Can't you write about Gran's dog?"

"That's no good," the twins said together. "We have to write about a pet that belongs to us. We need a pet and we want a dog."

"I want a frog and I'm not going to school," said David.

   "You will have to get up very early every day if
you have a dog," said Mum. "A dog needs a lot of
exercise. You will have to take it for a long run in
the woods every morning before breakfast.
It will be fun in the summer, but it will be cold and
wet and dark in the winter."

   "I want a frog," said David, banging his drum.

Andrew and Carol looked at each other.
They wanted a dog but they did not want
to go into the woods on cold, wet mornings.
Sometimes there were strange noises in the woods.
Some people thought witches lived there.
Of course, they didn't believe in witches,
but it wasn't worth taking any chances.
  "Well then," they said. "We'll have a hamster.
Lots of people in our class have hamsters."

"Yes," Mum said. "A hamster will be easier
to look after than a dog. But sometimes
hamsters get hungry and chew things that
aren't any good for them. You will have to be
very tidy and not leave any clothes or toys
on the floor if you have a hamster."

Carol and Andrew looked at each other again.
It would be difficult to be tidy all the time.
In fact, it was difficult to be tidy at all!

"I want another biscuit," sang David, banging his drum. "I want a frog, a dog and a monkey."

A monkey! Andrew and Carol looked at Mum. Mum looked at them.

"No!" she said. "I'm not having a monkey in the house. This isn't a jungle."

Carol said, "Jenny has a rabbit. It's white and silky and lovely to stroke. I'd like a rabbit."

"I like rabbits," said Mum, "and so do foxes. A rabbit has to live in a hutch outside. It would make a nice easy dinner for a hungry fox."

The twins thought about that. They had heard the foxes barking in the woods. They sounded fierce and very hungry. Perhaps it wasn't a good idea to have a rabbit.

David banged his drum and sang, "I want
a frog, a dog, a monkey and a tiger."

"Definitely no tigers!" said Mum. "No monkeys.
No tigers. But perhaps we could get
a cat, a striped cat." Then she looked at David.
"And no frogs either. Frogs don't live in houses.
But if you pick up all your crumbs we will go
to the pond and look for frogs."

Chapter 2: Striped cats and tigers

On the way to the pond, Andrew and Carol thought about a cat.

"How would we get one?" they asked. "Who sells cats? Who sells striped cats? Will it look a little bit like a tiger?"

At the pond David looked for frogs. He made so much noise the frogs stayed hidden. He looked up at the trees for monkeys. There weren't any. Then he crawled in the grass to look for tigers. There weren't any tigers either.

"If we get a cat, will there be lots to write about it?" Andrew asked.

"I don't think you can write about a cat unless you have a witch in the story," said Carol. "All the stories with cats have a witch. And I've written about a witch already."

"But witches have black cats," Andrew said. "If we get a striped cat, we can say it's a tiger. That might make things more interesting."

"David looks interesting," said Mum.

Everyone looked at David. He was very muddy and green in patches. Then Mum looked at the twins and said, "If we get a cat, you will have to look after it very carefully. We aren't getting a pet just for you to write about it in school. Now you think about that on the way home."

They were still thinking about it when
Mum came out of the bathroom with David.
He was very clean and very sleepy.

Mum said, "I'm going shopping tomorrow.
I could ask in the shops to see if anyone has
a striped cat." Then she looked at them hard.
"Of course, if you aren't going to school,
it will be difficult to go shopping. I won't
have time to ask about anything."

"All right," the twins said at last. "We'll go."

When they got on the bus the next morning,
Carol and Andrew shouted, "Remember our striped cat.
We're going to write all about him."

"We will," said Mum. "We'll do our best."

David called out, "A frog, a dog, a monkey and
a tiger," and banged his drum.
He banged it all the way to the shops and
he banged it when Mum asked about cats.

Chapter 3: The striped cat shop

When the bus came round the corner at four o'clock David was still banging his drum. He was also singing his song very loudly. "I want a frog, a dog, a monkey and a tiger."

"We don't," said Andrew and Carol as they got off the bus. "We want a striped cat. Have you found one?"

"No," said Mum, "but we're going to look for one now. We have to go to the R.S.P.C.A."

"What's that?" Carol asked.

"It's the striped cat shop," said Andrew.

"Not quite," said Mum. "It's the Royal Society for the Prevention of Cruelty to Animals. The people there sometimes look after stray animals. There are some kittens at our local branch. If we go now, we can look at the kittens and maybe choose one."

"We want a striped kitten," the twins sang
on the way to the R.S.P.C.A. David clapped
his hands and sang his own song.

Andrew knocked on the door of the R.S.P.C.A.
A lady opened it. She held a striped cat in her arms.

"Thank you," said Andrew and tried to take the cat.

"That's for us," Carol said and stroked the cat.
The lady looked very surprised.

She looked even more surprised when
David shouted, "Tiger."

"Please can we take it now?" the twins asked.

"No you can't," the lady replied. "What is this all about?"

Mum explained.

"Oh," said the lady. "Yes, we did have some striped kittens. They belonged to this cat. Someone found her near the main road and brought her to us. She had her kittens the very next day. But we've found homes for them. There's only one left."

"We'll have it," the twins said.

"You can look at it," said the lady. "But first
I want to look at you. Will you be good to it?
Do you know how to look after a kitten properly?
Will you promise not to tease it?"

"Yes, yes," the children shouted. "Now can we
look at it please?"

Chapter 4: The black kitten

They all went into the office and there
in the corner they saw the kitten.

"Tiger, tiger," shouted David.

But it wasn't. It was a tiny black kitten, just a
little scrap of black, glossy fur. The twins looked
at each other. They had written about a striped cat.
This little black kitten was no use. It was small and
weak and the wrong colour.

"Tiger, tiger," sang David softly.
The tiny black kitten heard him.
It stretched its back, then
it stretched its front paws. It opened
its eyes into two little shiny green slits, like emeralds.
The twins knelt down and stroked its glossy fur.
The kitten stretched again and
stuck out a little pink tongue.

"It needs a lot of looking after," the R.S.P.C.A. lady said. "Its mother isn't interested in it because it's so weak."

"It isn't green like a frog," said David.

"Be quiet David. There's no such thing as a green cat. It's a witch's cat," said Andrew.

Mum knelt down to stroke it with just one finger. The tiny black kitten uncurled and crept onto the palm of her hand. Andrew looked surprised. Perhaps Mum was a witch.

"I think we should wait for a striped cat,"
Mum said. The kitten curled up into a furry ball
on her hand and went to sleep.

"I know it isn't striped, but I quite like it,"
Andrew said.

"I think it's lovely," said Carol. "Someone
has to look after it if its mother doesn't
want it. There might not be anyone else
in the whole world who is looking for a pet."

"Well," said Mum. "I like black cats best of all."

"It might grow into a panther," Andrew said.
"A black panther is as good as a tiger."

The R.S.P.C.A. lady said, "It certainly seems
to like you. If you promise to take good care of it,
I could let you have it for a few days.
Then I will come and see if it is happy with you.
Remember though, no teasing."

Chapter 5: A cat called Tim

    Carol and Andrew pushed David home and
Mum carried the kitten very carefully in her hands.
    They put a saucer of milk onto the kitchen floor
and the kitten lapped it up with its rough pink tongue.
Then it went into the sitting room, curled up in a ball on
a cushion and went to sleep.
    Andrew and Carol watched it and began to plan
a story. They wrote it at school the next day . . .

The Black Panther

'Once upon a time there was a little black kitten.
He was so small and weak that nobody wanted him.
One day three children came looking for a cat.
They wanted a striped cat like a tiger but when
they saw the tiny black kitten they felt sorry for him.
They took him home and fed him.
They looked after him so well that he grew and
grew until he was as big as a panther.

"Now what will we do?" their Mum asked.
"This panther is too big for us.
We'll have to take him to the jungle."
So the children put a gold chain round
his neck and set out to find a jungle . . .'

That was the beginning of their story.
They had to stop writing then because it
was time to go home.

All the time Andrew and Carol were writing
their story at school, David was at home,
playing and singing. He sang his song
so many times that Mum shouted at him,
"For goodness sake. Stop singing those words.
Sing something different. Sing about a cat, a rat and
a chimpanzee."

They were just words that came into her head.
David liked the sound of them. He tried a new song.
He couldn't say chimpanzee. All he could say was
"Tim . . . tim . . . tim."

David liked his new song. "A cat, a rat and
a tim . . . tim . . . tim," he sang.
The tiny black kitten thought it was especially for him.
When Carol and Andrew came home they shouted,
"Where is Panther? We are going to
call him Panther."
But the kitten didn't answer. He didn't stretch.
He didn't yawn. He didn't open his green
emerald eyes. The only name he ever wanted was . . .
Tim.

Tim

Black cat
lies in the sun.
Tail curls,
green eyes blink,
pink tongue licks
glistening fur.

Black cat
prowls in the grass.
Tail flicks,
eyes glint,
ears twitch,
claws pounce.

Printed in Great Britain
by Amazon